[GUARDRAILS]

ANDY STANLEY

NP
NORTH POINT
RESOURCES

ZONDERVAN®

ZONDERVAN

Guardrails Study Guide, Updated Edition
Copyright © 2018 by North Point Ministries, Inc.

This title is also available as a Zondervan ebook.

Requests for information should be addressed to:
Zondervan, *3900 Sparks Dr. SE, Grand Rapids, Michigan 49546*

ISBN 978-0-310-09589-7

First Printing June 2018 / Printed in the United States of America

CONTENTS

USING THE STUDY GUIDE

BEFORE THE FIRST GROUP MEETING

 Read through the Introduction for an overview of the study.

 Flip through pages 9–19 to understand the layout of a session.

DURING EACH GROUP MEETING

 Turn to the Video Notes page and watch the video segment.

 Use the Discussion Questions to have a conversation about the video content.

 Review the Bottom Line at the end of the session.

AFTER EACH GROUP MEETING

 On your own, read and complete the challenge section.

2 Review the session recap at the end of each chapter.

INTRODUCTION

We've all seen guardrails on the shoulder of the highway. They exist to block our cars from straying into dangerous terrain. Most days, we don't even notice them.

But if you hit a slippery patch of road or have to drive a treacherous mountain pass, you're sure glad those guardrails are there. Yes, hitting one will do some damage—a busted fender or a dented door. But without the guardrail, the damage could be catastrophic.

Highways aren't the only place guardrails are helpful. Personal guardrails can keep you from straying into dangers that could damage your marriage, your finances, or your career.

Every day, you're navigating a wet, slippery road with disaster just one bad decision away. Return the call? Go to the party? Buy this? Say that? These seemingly unimportant decisions could have a huge impact on your future, and culture is baiting you toward the wrong choices. It romanticizes the idea of living for the moment—of doing what you want, with whomever you want, whenever you want.

Without guardrails, you're exposed to the danger. One day, you may be left with catastrophic damage to clean up.

Establishing boundaries for how you behave at work, how you spend your money, and how you manage your relationships can protect you. Just like hitting a guardrail with your car, bumping into your personal guardrails may leave your career, your bank account, or your relationship with a few dents, but it will keep you from careening off the edge.

So, let's stop flirting with disaster. Let's set up the protection we need. No one regrets having guardrails in place. But plenty of us look back and regret not having them.

[DIRECT AND PROTECT]

We're all aware of the destructive consequences associated with poor decisions or lapses in judgment. We don't plan to mess up. But it can easily happen if we try to navigate life without guardrails.

It's not enough to hope God will protect us. He doesn't usually keep us from the consequences of decisions we make freely. His protection comes when we seek and apply the wisdom he's provided in the Bible—wisdom that is the basis for all personal guardrails.

God isn't being cruel or mean. He has given us the freedom to live as we choose. But he has also defined guardrails that lead us toward peace and contentment and away from regret.

VIDEO NOTES

DISCUSSION QUESTIONS

1 Andy suggests that *culture doesn't encourage guardrails; culture is content with painted lines.* Then he offered a few "painted-line" examples:

- Drink responsibly.
- Wait till you're ready.
- Consolidate your debts.
- Listen to your heart.

Have you ever considered these examples to be mixed messages?

2 Why do you think culture resists rules?

3 Have you ever heard of the "Billy Graham rule"—more recently known as the "Mike Pence rule"? The male Christian leaders that adhere to this practice avoid spending car rides, work trips, and meals alone with women other than their spouses. Billy Graham and Mike Pence adopted the rule to safeguard their marriages and reputations.

What is your initial reaction to this rule? Good idea? Too extreme?

4 Have you ever been criticized for setting standards or establishing boundaries?

5 In Ephesians 5:17, Paul writes, "Therefore do not be foolish, but understand what the Lord's will is." The Greek translation of the verb "to understand" means to face up to, to acknowledge, to be honest with yourself, to stop deceiving yourself.

Why is it so difficult to be honest about (to understand) where we need wisdom and guardrails in our lives?

 6 Ephesians 5:15–16 reads, "Be very careful, then, how you live—not as unwise but as wise, making the most of every opportunity, because the days are evil." Is there a choice or regret you could have avoided if you were more careful about how you lived?

THIS WEEK'S CHALLENGE

Now it's time to take action. Guardrails only direct and protect you if you take steps to establish them.

Your answers to the following two questions are just for you. You don't have to share them with anyone. But if there's someone in your group or in your life who can support, encourage, and pray for you as you move toward establishing a new guardrail, consider talking to that person.

What is one area of your life in which you need to establish or strengthen some guardrails? Identify that area in the space below:

- ☐ Finances (e.g., money)
- ☐ Relationships (e.g., marriage)
- ☐ Morals (e.g., values)
- ☐ Profession (e.g., coworkers)
- ☐ Other: _____

What is a first step you can take this week to begin establishing a new guardrail in that area?

SESSION RECAP

Self-restraint isn't fun. We all want to do what we want to do, when we want to do it. But self-restraint keeps us out of trouble. The idea of guardrails isn't new. It's been around for a long time. In fact, the Hebrew Bible—what we call our Old Testament—talks about setting standards and boundaries. The New Testament talks about the same thing. In his letter to the people at the church of Ephesus, the apostle Paul wrote:

> *Be very careful, then, how you live—not as unwise but as wise, making the most of every opportunity, because the days are evil. Therefore do not be foolish, but understand what the Lord's will is. Do not get drunk on wine, which leads to debauchery. Instead, be filled with the Spirit...*
>
> **EPHESIANS 5:15-18**

This is great advice, whether or not you're a Jesus follower: "Be very careful then, how you live." The Greek word translated "live" actually means "walk." Paul wants us to be aware of what's happening around us because being aware of trouble is the first step in avoiding it.

When Paul uses the word "wisdom" in the verse, he's talking about more than *knowing* right from wrong. Wisdom is about making decisions in your daily life. It's about recognizing what action has the best *long-term* outcome for you and then following through on that action. It means asking this question:

> **"In light of my past experience, my current circumstances, and my future hopes and dreams, what is the wise thing for me to do?"**

Paul also recommends "making the most of every opportunity." That's because you know you have a limited amount of time, but you don't know how much time you have. It's tempting to live as though you have all the time in the world, but the risk you run is wasting opportunities you've been given.

Don't you wish you could go back and get a do-over on some of the time you wasted? Most of us feel that way. We wish we could do our freshman year over again, or our first year of marriage, or our first year in that job we didn't really like. Paul reminds us that we already know what happens when we're not careful with our time. So, don't live as unwise but as wise. Pay attention to how fast time passes.

Why? "Because the days are evil." That means you have to pay attention to what others are doing, because their choices can affect your life, for good or bad. Think of it this way: when you were learning to drive, you were told that by paying attention to what other drivers were doing, you would minimize the danger they posed to you or your vehicle.

[That's wisdom.]

Wisdom says you can't approach life as if what happened yesterday doesn't affect today and what happens today doesn't affect tomorrow.

Paul wrote, "Therefore, do not be foolish, but understand what the Lord's will is." That statement can be confusing. Isn't God's will mysterious? Paul's point is that we have enormous capacity for self-deception. If we want something, even if we know it isn't wise, we can find all sorts of ways to rationalize our desire. But ignoring wisdom to get what we want is foolish and dangerous. It's also against God's will because he doesn't want you to "suffer harm."

Deep down, you know the wise thing to do. You know the world in which you live. You know your past and your propensity toward certain habits and behaviors. Wisdom requires you to be honest with the person in the mirror. Do the wise thing.

That's what guardrails are all about. They safeguard us from handing over control of our lives to someone or something else.

The New Testament teaches that when a person puts their faith in Jesus, the Holy Spirit comes to reside in them in a mysterious way. The Holy Spirit empowers that person to live wisely. So, instead of giving control of your life to anything or anyone—alcohol, work, finances, greed, a hobby, a person, an affair—submit your life to the nudging of the Holy Spirit.

GUARDRAILS SAFEGUARD YOU FROM HANDING OVER CONTROL OF YOUR LIFE TO SOMEONE OR SOMETHING ELSE.

[PROXIMITY]

Have you ever met someone you later wished you hadn't?

Your greatest regrets are usually associated with people in one way or another. Either you regret a relationship, or you regret the influence someone had over you. That may sound judgmental, but it's not. It's showing good judgment.

Being judgmental is when you draw a harsh or critical conclusion about someone else. It's when you expect another person to be or act like someone they aren't. Showing good judgment is when you draw a conclusion about *yourself* based on wisdom. It's when you choose to make a course correction based on the answer to the question, "In light of my past experience, current circumstances, and future hopes and dreams, what is the wise thing to do?"

VIDEO NOTES

DISCUSSION QUESTIONS

 How would you define being *judgmental* versus having *good judgment*?

 Solomon wrote, "Walk with the wise and become wise, for a companion of fools suffers harm" (Proverbs 13:20). Is there a wise person who has influenced you for the better?

 Has there been a case where you have suffered harm from a bad friendship or relationship?

During the video, Andy said, "Friends can be dangerous. And danger requires guardrails. You need to establish a standard that informs your conscience." The following are five guardrails he suggested for relationships.

- When it dawns on you your core group isn't moving in the direction you want to be moving...

- When you catch yourself trying to be someone you aren't...

- When you feel pressure to compromise...

- When you catch yourself thinking, *I'll go, but I won't participate*...

- When you hope the people you care about don't know your whereabouts...

Can you think of a time when one of these guardrails lit up your conscience? How did you respond?

 Do you have an example of a time when you had to enforce a guardrail in a friendship? How did it turn out?

THIS WEEK'S CHALLENGE

Name a person who currently influences you to make wise decisions.

What is one thing you can do to dial up that person's influence in your life? Be specific.

....

....

....

....

....

....

....

....

Accept the challenge. Follow through on the action you wrote down. It's a great way to begin establishing relational guardrails.

SESSION RECAP

You may not know this, but you are an acceptance magnet. We're all acceptance magnets. It's human nature. We're drawn to whichever groups of people accept us as we are. But acceptance isn't the best measure for choosing our friends.

You've probably seen someone join a group of friends that exerted a negative influence on them. Suddenly, that person was making unwise choices—choices that seemed out of character. Maybe that's even been you.

When it comes to relationships, we need to be on our guard. *We need guardrails.*

If you want to maximize happiness and minimize stress, you have to be intentional about surrounding yourself with people who embody the traits you want to create in your own life. That's because, as neuroscientist and Northwestern University professor Moran Cerf said,* "The more we study engagement, we see time and time again that just being next to certain people actually aligns your brain with them. This isn't just behavioral. This is neurological."

> *You are wired to be influenced by the people who have the closest proximity to you. The people you do life with will influence your future.*

About three thousand years ago, a man named Solomon was ancient Israel's third king. He is most famous, even today, for his great wisdom. In fact, some of the wisest passages in the Old Testament are credited to him. Here's what Solomon wrote: "Walk with the wise and become wise, for a companion of fools suffers harm" (Proverbs 13:20).

If you "walk with the wise," you will probably, without effort or intentionality, become wise. You won't have to study or write anything down. It'll just happen over time. And who is a wise person? Somebody who understands that life is connected— your past connects to your present, which is a predictor of your future.

There's a second part of the verse: "for a companion of fools suffers harm." We don't really call people fools anymore, but in the Scriptures, a fool is a person who lives for the moment. They don't consider the past or plan for tomorrow. They aren't careful.

The interesting thing is what Solomon wrote about hanging out with fools. If you walk with the wise, he says you become wise. So, you expect him to say if you're a companion of fools, you will become a fool. Instead, he says something far worse will happen. If you hang out with fools, you will *suffer harm*. When their lives go bad, your life will be negatively affected because of your proximity. The closer you are to them, the worse it will be for you because when their lives blow up, you will be in range of the shrapnel.

> *Friends who aren't careful with their health won't be concerned with your health. Friends who aren't careful with their marriages won't guard your marriage. Friends who aren't careful with their finances won't positively influence your finances. Friends who aren't concerned with their reputations won't protect your reputation. Friends who don't have any kind of faith won't want to bother with your faith. And friends who don't care about their own futures won't worry about your future.*

So, here are five guidelines for establishing guardrails in your friendships. Your conscience should light up when...

 It dawns on you that your core group isn't moving in the direction you want to be moving.

 You catch yourself trying to be someone you aren't.

3 You feel pressure to compromise.

4 You catch yourself thinking, *I'll go, but I won't participate.*

5 You hope the people you care about don't know your whereabouts.

*businessinsider.com/neuroscientist-most-important-choice-in-life-2017-7

[

**FRIENDS WHO
DON'T TAKE
CARE OF**
THEMSELVES
**WON'T TAKE
CARE OF** YOU.

]

[FOREVER YOURS]

We entertain ourselves with media that glorifies infidelity and sex outside of marriage. Yet nearly everyone (Christians and non-Christians alike) agrees that it's immoral to use others sexually and to break our commitments to those we love.

When we discover a friend has had an affair, we're mortified. That kind of behavior is fun and exciting when we see it in movies or on television, but we're disgusted by it in real life. That disconnect between how we view life and the media we consume sets us up to veer over the edge into the danger zone in our own lives.

Sexual immorality has huge consequences for our society. It contributes to things such as poverty, unwanted pregnancies, and domestic violence. Imagine how our world might change if we established some personal guardrails in this area.

VIDEO NOTES

DISCUSSION QUESTIONS

 Due to the sensitivity of the content discussed this week, we recommend splitting the group by gender for video viewing and discussion.

 People define "fidelity"/"faithfulness" in a variety of ways. In reference to a romantic relationship, how would you define it?

 Paul wrote in 1 Corinthians 6:18 that we should "flee sexual immorality." How does culture bait people to *flirt with* rather than *flee from* sexual immorality?

During the video, Andy defined "sin" as "hurting, stealing from, or dishonoring someone." Is this different from or similar to how you've historically thought about sin?

 Do you agree that sexual sin can make someone a secret keeper for life? Why do people often choose to keep their sexual sin hidden?

5 Andy offered three steps when it comes to creating and enforcing guardrails. Do you think these steps work in real life? Why or why not?

A. Talk about it with _____.

(Hint: Who can offer a safe sounding board for discussing potential areas where guardrails may be needed?)

☐ Small group
☐ Trusted advisor
☐ Counselor
☐ Other: _____

B. Tell _____ about it.

(Hint: What relationship is this guardrail protecting? Be forthcoming—tell the person you have decided to put this guardrail in place. This will keep you accountable.)

☐ Spouse
☐ Significant other
☐ Other: _____

C. Tell _____ before you cross the guardrail.

(Hint: Do you have a safe person, maybe in this group, whom you could trust when you're tempted to step over a guardrail?)

☐ Trusted friend
☐ Mentor
☐ Pastor
☐ Other: _____

THIS WEEK'S CHALLENGE

When it comes to sexuality and attraction, what is one thing you can do this week to firm up a guardrail or establish a new guardrail?

Sex is a sensitive subject. It often stirs feelings of shame and regret. But you're more likely to follow through on establishing a guardrail if you have the support of another person. If you're not comfortable sharing your struggles in this area with the group, is there a person you do trust to support and encourage you? Would you reach out to them?

SESSION RECAP

Two thousand years ago, the apostle Paul was planting little churches all around the Mediterranean Rim. He wrote a letter to a church in the city of Corinth in Greece. He'd already been there and taught the people in the church. But he wrote this letter to remind them of what they already knew.

> *Flee from sexual immorality. All other sins a person commits are outside the body, but whoever sins sexually, sins against their own body. Do you not know that your bodies are temples of the Holy Spirit, who is in you, whom you have received from God? You are not your own; you were bought at a price. Therefore honor God with your bodies.*
>
> **1 CORINTHIANS 6:18–20**

In our culture, this sounds extreme. But isn't it exactly what every husband wants his wife to do? Isn't it exactly what every wife wants her husband to do? Isn't it what every parent wants their teenager or young adult to do? When it comes to sexuality, we want the people we love to be careful. We know carelessness in this area can lead to life-altering consequences.

But our culture often treats sex as a disposable commodity. We continually receive the message that sex is just physical. It's no big deal as long as it's between consenting adults. We're encouraged to flirt with sexual immorality instead of running away from it. Many movies and TV shows treat marital infidelity like it's inevitable and maybe even fun. Stories about affairs sell. But when a celebrity is caught cheating in real life, their reputation is torn down in the media.

So, we allow ourselves to be baited to the edge of disaster, and when we step off that edge, we feel shame. Or we condemn other people who step off that edge. Why do we run toward fictitious stories of sexual immorality but condemn it when we see it, even from afar, in real life? Why do we entertain infidelity as something exciting and dramatic when we know it actually hurts people?

The apostle Paul told followers of Jesus to *flee* from sexual immorality.

When he wrote, "All other sins a person commits are outside the body, but whoever sins sexually, sins against their own body," he put sexual sin in a category of its own. That's not because sexual sin is unforgivable. It's because it's uniquely damaging. You can never fully escape the consequences of that sin. Sexual immorality undermines future intimacy to one extent or another. It has a way of continuing to resurface.

Sexual sin can make you a liar and a secret keeper. You'll admit other kinds of sin but hide sexual sin. Some of the most brokenhearted people are those who married only to later discover that their spouses hid part of their sexual histories. The spouses shared enough to relieve their consciences but didn't tell the whole story. They made promises to the most important people in their lives, but kept secrets they were too ashamed to tell. Eventually, that secrecy and shame blew up in their marriages.

So, when we talk about sexual "sin," what exactly do we mean? It's a religious-sounding word, but the New Testament offers a simple definition. Sin is hurting another person. Anytime I put me before you to your detriment, it's a sin. God loves *every person*, so we don't get a pass on hurting *anyone*.

The standard of living for followers of Jesus is the Platinum Rule. You've heard of the Golden Rule: "Do unto others as you would have them do unto you." But the Platinum Rule is an even higher standard:

[*"Treat others the way God, through Christ, has treated you."*]

That means followers of Jesus should put others ahead of themselves even when those others don't deserve it. Why? Because that's what Jesus did for us.

So, sexual sin isn't sin because God has something against sex. It's sin because God loves the people you hurt and he loves you. God doesn't want you to hurt you. When you take sex—an extraordinary gift designed for an exclusive relationship with another person—and divvy it up among numerous other relationships, you not only hurt those people, you hurt yourself.

When Paul wrote about sexual sin, this is why he shifted the conversation from consequence to identity. He wrote, "Do you not know that your bodies are temples of the Holy Spirit, who is in you, whom you have received from God? You are not your own; you were bought at a price."

That passage may sound strange and religious to you, but Paul is simply saying that you are fine-tuned for a relationship with God *and* relationships with others. Fleeing from sexual immorality isn't about being a "good Christian" by rejecting everything that's fun and feels good. It's about maximizing your capacity for healthy relationships by enabling you to treat others the way God treated you.

Your sexuality can be a wonderful gift. It can also be a danger zone. If you stray into that danger zone, it can undermine your relationship with God by harming others and yourself. It can leave you with a lifetime of regret.

YOU ARE A SACRED IMAGE BEARER... AND THE VALUE OF A CONTAINER IS DETERMINED BY WHAT IT CONTAINS.

[MONEY MATTERS]

When it comes to your finances, God wants something *for* you, not *from* you.

Establishing financial guardrails isn't about staying out of debt. It's not about how to avoid bankruptcy. It's not about creating a sound retirement plan.

It's about something much deeper. It's about freedom.

According to Jesus, it doesn't matter how much money you have. What matters is having financial guardrails in place so you are in charge of your money and it's not in charge of you.

VIDEO NOTES

DISCUSSION QUESTIONS

1 On a typical day, how often do you think about money?

2 During the video, Andy defined "greed" as "an assumption that it's all for my consumption." Do you agree with that definition? Why or why not?

3 Read Matthew 6:25–27.

> *"Do not worry about your life, what you will eat or drink; or about your body, what you will wear. Is not life more than food, and the body more than clothes? Look at the birds of the air; they do not sow or reap or store away in barns, and yet your heavenly Father feeds them. Are you not much more valuable than they? Can any one of you by worrying add a single hour to your life?"*

Why is it challenging to *not worry* about money?

What increases *worry* about money?

Why is it often difficult for people to believe that God and the church want something *for* them and not money *from* them?

 What obstacles have, in the past or present, prevented you from giving first, saving second, and living off the rest? What would keep you from prioritizing giving moving forward?

THIS WEEK'S CHALLENGE

This week, set aside a couple of hours to take a detailed look at your budget for last month. Put every dollar into the Give, Save, or Live category.

GIVE	SAVE	LIVE

Use the pie chart below to draw the percentage of your income that went to each category. Then answer the questions underneath the pie chart.

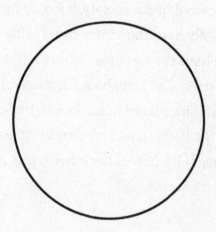

 Are you satisfied with where your money is currently going?

2 If you want to increase the percentage allocated to one category, how will you decrease it in others? What actions can you take to begin to make those adjustments?

SESSION RECAP

Greed is a dirty word in our society, but only because we define it as actively harming others by refusing to meet their needs when we have the resources to do so. But that definition is too narrow. Greed isn't just about harming others. It's the assumption that if it's placed in my hands, it's for me. If it goes in my 401(k), it's for me. If it's part of my paycheck or my bonus, it's for me. If it's part of my inheritance, it's for me. If I win the lottery, it's for me.

[
Greed is an assumption that it's all for my consumption.
]

That assumption can lead to a "consume now" mentality. The tragedy is that when you live that way, you live as if there is no God. You live as if this life is all there is. You might as well eat, drink, and be merry because tomorrow you will die. And then it's over. Who cares about your legacy? You're gone.

But if there is something in you that thinks, *There must be more to this life*, then don't allow your life to be driven by consumption or hoarding. Don't live as if there is no God. Don't live as if it's all about you.

When you live as if there is no God, trouble eventually comes along and causes you to reevaluate your choices. You bought too much house, leased too much car, or took out too many loans. Or maybe somebody laid you off, lied to you, or took the money and ran. And when trouble comes along, as it does for all of us, what do we do? We pray.

It may be a whispered prayer on the way to the bank or a full-throated, "Oh, God, please rescue me!" Either way, we invite God into our finances when we have problems. We offer an invitation to our heavenly Father when we need a job, a consolidation loan, mercy at work, or a little grace on the mortgage payment.

So, the question is, if you would pray and invite God into your finances when there's a problem, why not invite him in now, *before* there's a problem? The way you do that is by reprioritizing your finances. If you're like most people, you live on the first portion of your earnings, you save a little, and then, if there's any money left over, you might give. Your top priority is spending your money on you. That's human nature—me first, me second, and then everybody else.

But if you don't want your finances to master you, flip the order. Give first, save next, and live on the rest. When you prioritize your finances that way, it breaks money's control over your life. It prevents you from living as though there is no God.

Jesus addressed this idea in the gospel of Matthew:

> *"No one can serve two masters. Either you will hate the one and love the other, or you will be devoted to the one and despise the other. You cannot serve both God and money."*
>
> *"So do not worry, saying, 'What shall we eat?' or 'What shall we drink?' or 'What shall we wear?' For the pagans run after all these things, and your heavenly Father knows that you need them. But seek first his kingdom and his righteousness, and all these things will be given to you as well."*
>
> **MATTHEW 6:24, 31-33**

You can't be a slave to consumption *and* serve God. It's impossible.

Jesus knows our inclination is to worry about our money. So, he reminds us that God knows what we need. And when we believe that strongly enough to live as though it's true, God replaces money as our master.

The moment you wrap your heart and your belief system around the truth that God knows what you need, you will begin to build your capacity to live with your hands wide open. And when you live with your hands wide open, you're able to prioritize others' *needs* over your *wants*. You're able to trust that your generosity toward others today won't turn into regret tomorrow.

That kind of trust begins with a simple but powerful truth: *everything you have belongs to God.* You don't own it, but he's given you an opportunity to manage it in a way that demonstrates your trust in him and your love for other people.

The way you do that is to establish guardrails against greed:

- Give first—prioritize others over yourself.
- Save second—make sure you're prepared when trouble arrives.
- Live on what's left.

[DO YOU HAVE MONEY OR DOES MONEY HAVE YOU?]

[THE HEART OF THE MATTER]

The point of guardrails is to light up our consciences before we hurt ourselves or other people. They prompt us to feel uneasy before it's too late.

Solomon, the second king of Israel and considered in ancient times the wisest person who ever lived, wrote this in the Old Testament book of Proverbs: "Above all else, guard your heart, for everything you do flows from it" (Proverbs 4:23).

Our hearts determine the quality of our relationship with God and other people. They determine the quality of our lives. At least that's what Solomon believed. What if he was right?

VIDEO NOTES

DISCUSSION QUESTIONS

1 When have you seen someone blow up or lose it over something inconsequential? Knowing that "what comes out of the mouth flows from the heart," what do you think could have really been going on?

2 Proverbs 4:23 says, "Above all else, guard your heart, for everything you do flows from it." What are some examples of ways "your heart" fuels how you react or behave?

3 Jesus stated in Matthew 15:18, "But the things that come out of a person's mouth come from the heart, and these defile them." The relationship between our hearts and our actions is explained with a visual below. Before today's video teaching, had you considered that your negative behavior is offensive to God?

MY HEART

⌄

MY NEGATIVE BEHAVIORS

⌄

OFFENDS PEOPLE

⋯⋯⋯⋯> **OFFENDS GOD**

(because God loves the offended people)

4 Which of the four emotions Andy mentioned is your biggest tendency? Do you relate to any of the "owe" statements?

☐ Guilt *(I owe you.)*
☐ Anger *(You owe me.)*
☐ Greed *(I owe me.)*
☐ Jealousy *(Life owes me.)*

If you feel comfortable doing so, talk to the group about why you selected the statement(s) you did.

5 Andy proposed that some of the people we respect the most are the ones who have endured suffering and pain but have refused to be owned by anger or resentment. Why are those people so impressive?

THIS WEEK'S CHALLENGE

Take a few minutes to read through the list of heart sicknesses Andy mentioned in the video. Are you experiencing any of them?

- ☐ Guilt *(I owe you.)*
- ☐ Anger *(You owe me.)*
- ☐ Greed *(I owe me.)*
- ☐ Jealousy *(Life owes me.)*

Four preventative exercises were proposed to help you take steps toward a healed heart. Circle one of the **BOLDED** actions that would be a step toward healing for you.

Guilt ·············> **CONFESS** _____

Anger ·············> **FORGIVE** _____

Greed ·············> **GIVE** _____

Jealousy ·············> **CELEBRATE** _____

Who can you reach out to for encouragement and support in this area?

71

SESSION RECAP

The most important guardrail is the one that protects your heart. If you don't deal with what's on the inside, it eventually makes its way to the outside. And when it does, it will not only hurt you but also the people you love most.

That's offensive to God because he loves the people you hurt and he loves you.

As you wrap up this study, let's talk about four emotions that should ding your conscience. When you feel one of them, it should cause you to pause. It should be a warning sign that you have some work to do. These emotions are indicators that it's time to establish or reestablish some guardrails. They are:

Guilt (I owe you.)

Anger (You owe me.)

Greed (I owe me.)

Jealousy (Life owes me.)

Don't let these emotions fester. When you feel them, take immediate action to address the internal tension.

Guilt says, "I owe you because I took something from you." It creates distance and leads to keeping secrets. It seeps into your words and makes its way into your relationships.

Anger says, "You owe me because you took something from me. You either pay me back or I will pay you back." The problem with anger is that it leaks. It's never isolated to the relationship of its origin. If you were hurt as a kid or in that last job or in that last relationship, you carry that hurt into adulthood or the next job or the next relationship.

Greed says, "I owe me." We talked about this last session. It's the assumption that all you have is for your consumption. When you're greedy, the people closest to you feel like they're competing with your stuff. They feel less important than the car or house. When you like nice stuff more than you like other people, it's a problem. It should bother you.

Jealousy says, "Life owes me. Somebody else got what I deserved." And now you don't like that person. It's almost impossible to be nice to them. You resent what they have because you believe it should be yours.

When you feel these emotions—and we all feel them sometimes—you have to address them right away. These four preventative heart exercises will keep you out of a ditch. They are the opposite of what you feel like doing when you're experiencing negative emotions, but they'll keep you in the safe zone.

When you feel guilt, confess. And don't just confess to God. If you feel like you owe someone because you took something from them, confess to that person. That kind of confession has the power to heal guilt. It's a guardrail for your heart.

When you feel anger, forgive. Forgiveness is identifying what was taken from you and deciding the other person doesn't owe you anymore. It's not enough to say you had a terrible father or mother or boss. Identify what that person took from you. Be specific. Then decide to cancel the debt. That's what forgiveness is. It's hard and it takes time and effort. But it ensures that anger doesn't poison the other relationships in your life.

When you feel greed, give. Write some big checks (whatever "big" means to you). Give to a nonprofit. Give to a church. If you want to get serious, sell something precious to you and give the money away. Give as radically as you need to in order to break money's control over you.

When you feel jealousy, celebrate. Begin by celebrating what God has given you, and then celebrate what God has given others. Congratulate your coworker on that promotion you wanted. Be happy for the nicer, bigger house your friend just bought. Celebrate your sister's pregnancy even as you struggle with infertility. There's a fake-it-until-you-make-it aspect to that kind of celebration. But if you do it, you'll put jealousy on notice that it is not welcome to live in your heart. And eventually, your celebration will become genuine.

What's in your heart eventually shows up in your life. If you do these four preventative heart exercises, you'll experience what the apostle Paul described in his letter to the Philippians:

"And the peace of God, which transcends all understanding, will guard your hearts and your minds in Christ Jesus."

(PHILIPPIANS 4:7)

[**YOUR** BEHAVIOR **WILL EVENTUALLY** MIRROR **YOUR** HEART.]

[LEADING THE DISCUSSION]

If you are the lead facilitator of the Discussion Questions, here are three things to consider during your group meetings:

1 CULTIVATE DISCUSSION.

It's the ideas of everyone in the group that make a meeting successful. Your role as a facilitator is to create an environment in which people feel safe to share their thoughts.

2 STAY ON TRACK.

While you want to leave space for group members to think through the discussion, make sure the conversation is contributing to the topic. Don't let it veer off on tangents. Go with the flow, but be ready to nudge the conversation in the right direction when necessary.

3 PRAY.

This is the most important thing you can do as a leader. Pray that God is not only present at your group meetings but that he is directing them.

A TYPICAL GROUP MEETING

SOCIAL TIME	*30 minutes*
VIDEO	*30 minutes*
DISCUSSION	*50 minutes*
PRAYER	*10 minutes*

SESSION ONE
NOTES FOR LEADING

BOTTOM LINE

Just as we need physical guardrails on a road to direct and protect us, we need guardrails in other areas of our lives as well.

TO PREPARE TO LEAD THE FIRST SESSION:

- Read Ephesians 5:15–18, and use the following "Reflection" and "Prayer" sections to consider the verses you've read.

- Read the session materials, watch the video, and look through the Discussion Questions.

REFLECTION

As you read this week's verses, think about times when you've been foolish and times when you've understood God's will for your life. How were your circumstances different in each instance? What were you doing or not doing that made it easier for you to recognize God's will?

Remember: Just as we need physical guardrails on a road to direct and protect us, we need guardrails in other areas of our lives as well.

PRAYER

Spend some time this week reflecting on the role regret plays in your life. Also think about instances in which wisdom directed your decision-making and protected you from danger. Consider that regret may be playing a significant role in the lives of some of your group members. Express gratitude to God for his love for us and the wisdom he's provided. Ask him to soften your heart so you can provide encouragement and support to your group in the weeks to come.

NOTES FOR DISCUSSION QUESTIONS

 Andy suggests that culture doesn't encourage guardrails; culture is content with painted lines. Then he offered a few "painted-line" examples:

- *Drink responsibly.*
- *Wait till you're ready.*
- *Consolidate your debts.*
- *Listen to your heart.*

Have you ever considered these examples to be mixed messages?

This question is designed to get the group thinking about the session topic as well as their own assumptions about culture and faith. Treat the discussion as an open forum. It's okay if group members don't agree with Andy's premise. This is just the beginning of your conversation.

2 *Why do you think culture resists rules?*

Let your group brainstorm. The more ideas they come up with, the more fruitful the rest of the conversation will be.

3 *Have you ever heard of the "Billy Graham rule"—more recently known as the "Mike Pence rule"? The male Christian leaders that adhere to this practice avoid spending car rides, work trips, and meals alone with women other than their spouses. Billy Graham and Mike Pence adopted the rule to safeguard their marriages and reputations.*

What is your initial reaction to this rule? Good idea? Too extreme?

This question may generate a lot of disagreement. That's okay. Be open to others' perspectives, and don't worry about trying to change anyone's mind. Model curiosity and acceptance to the group by asking follow-up questions like, "What experiences have shaped your views on this topic?" or "Do you think the opposing view might be helpful to some people?"

 Have you ever been criticized for setting standards or establishing boundaries?

This is the first personal question. Be ready with your own example in case you need to encourage your group to open up. Remember to thank people for sharing.

5 *In Ephesians 5:17, Paul writes, "Therefore do not be foolish, but understand what the Lord's will is." The Greek translation of the verb "to understand" means to face up to, to acknowledge, to be honest with yourself, to stop deceiving yourself.*

Why is it so difficult to be honest about (to understand) where we need wisdom and guardrails in our lives?

As you prepare to lead this session, spend some time thinking about the barriers that prevent you from being honest with yourself. Be specific during your group discussion. Your vulnerability will encourage others to open up.

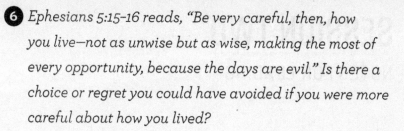

6 *Ephesians 5:15–16 reads, "Be very careful, then, how you live—not as unwise but as wise, making the most of every opportunity, because the days are evil." Is there a choice or regret you could have avoided if you were more careful about how you lived?*

Keep in mind that this is a challenging personal question. It's difficult for people to talk openly about their regrets. Create a safe environment by listening carefully, asking follow-up questions, and thanking people for their willingness to share.

SESSION TWO

NOTES FOR LEADING

BOTTOM LINE

Friends still influence the direction and quality of your life.

TO PREPARE TO LEAD THE SECOND SESSION:

- Read Proverbs 13:20 and Luke 7:35. Use the "Reflection" and "Prayer" sections to consider the verses you've read.

- Read the session materials, watch the video, and look through the Discussion Questions.

REFLECTION

Consider the ways you've benefited from walking with wise friends and have suffered harm as a result of walking with "fools."

Remember: Friends *still* influence the direction and quality of your life.

PRAYER

Spend time praying about your relationships. Ask God to help you recognize the influence, both positive and negative, they have on your life.

Also pray that your group members are able to reflect honestly on their past and present relationships. Ask God to help them see how they are acceptance magnets and help them begin to establish relational guardrails so they can make wise decisions.

NOTES FOR DISCUSSION QUESTIONS

 How would you define the difference between being judgmental and having good judgment?

Allow your group the space to brainstorm answers. This question is designed to set up the rest of the conversation, so it's not important that they come up with the correct response.

 Solomon wrote, "Walk with the wise and become wise, for a companion of fools suffers harm" (Proverbs 13:20). Is there a wise person who has influenced you for the better?

Be ready with your own answer. Be specific about what made the person wise and how you benefited from that wisdom.

Has there been a case where you have suffered harm from a bad friendship or relationship?

It can be difficult for people to share examples of their failures. Be encouraging. Withhold judgment. Offer an example from your past.

4 *During the video, Andy said, "Friends can be dangerous. And danger requires guardrails. You need to establish a standard that informs your conscience." The following are five guardrails he suggested for relationships.*

This question is relatively safe because it allows group members to talk about what they have observed in others. If you want to try to take the conversation to a deeper level, offer an example of a guardrail that *you* sometimes ignore or blow past.

 Do you have an example of a time when you had to enforce a guardrail in a friendship? How did it turn out?

Encourage people to answer by listening well and thanking them for their input. Don't pressure people to answer. Lead the way by being open and transparent in your answer.

SESSION THREE
NOTES FOR LEADING

BOTTOM LINE

Dangerous environments call for extreme measures. Morally dangerous environments call for guardrails.

TO PREPARE TO LEAD THE THIRD SESSION:

- Read 1 Corinthians 6:18–20 and use the "Reflection" and "Prayer" sections to consider the verses you've read.

- Read the session materials, watch the video, and look through the Discussion Questions.

REFLECTION

Life without guardrails in the area of sexuality can be particularly dangerous because we're all prone to keeping secrets when it comes to sex. Those secrets can cause shame, which festers and affects the quality of our other relationships.

Remember: Dangerous environments call for extreme measures. Morally dangerous environments call for guardrails.

PRAYER

Are you currently living with secrets? Have you prayed that God would help you break bad habits and free you from shame? If so, understand that you can't win this battle on your own. Pray that God will give you the courage and determination to open up to a trusted friend. Ask him to remind you that when we share our secrets, it breaks their power over us.

NOTES FOR DISCUSSION QUESTIONS

 People define "fidelity"/"faithfulness" in a variety of ways. In reference to a romantic relationship, how would you define it?

This can be a helpful question to begin to gauge your group members' reactions to this topic. Don't challenge or critique perspectives that differ from yours. Be patient. Allow the conversation to develop, and give your group members space to consider or reconsider their beliefs and assumptions.

 Paul wrote in 1 Corinthians 6:18 that we should "flee sexual immorality." How does culture bait people to flirt with rather than flee from sexual immorality?

Allow the group to come up with as many answers as they can. It will create a better discussion as the questions get deeper and more personal.

 During the video, Andy defined sin as "hurting, stealing from, or dishonoring someone." Is this different from or similar to how you've historically thought about sin?

Don't shortchange the discussion by rushing through this question. Group members' perspectives on sin are important and can vary greatly depending on their church backgrounds and where they are in their faith. Listen carefully. Ask follow-up questions if it's helpful. Resist the urge to correct.

 Do you agree that sexual sin can make someone a secret keeper for life? Why do people often choose to keep their sexual sin hidden?

This question invites disagreement. Allow the group space to disagree. Offer your own perspective (after you've listened), but without judgment or correction.

5 *Andy offered three steps when it comes to creating and enforcing guardrails. Do you think these steps work in real life? Why or why not?*

Give your group members a few minutes to review the three steps included in this question. Invite people to share their answers. Keep in mind that, for many people, establishing guardrails in this area is more difficult than other areas. Be ready to camp out on this question for a while. If someone selects "small group" under the first step, commit to following up with that person. Make sure you help create an environment where they feel safe to open up.

SESSION 4

NOTES FOR LEADING

BOTTOM LINE

Establish guardrails against greed. To avoid greed and irresponsibility: Give. Save. Live.

TO PREPARE TO LEAD THE FOURTH SESSION:

- Read Matthew 6:24, 31–33 and Mark 10:42–45. Use the "Reflection" and "Prayer" sections to consider the verses you've read.

- Read the session materials, watch the video, and look through the Discussion Questions.

REFLECTION

As you read the verses this week, ask yourself this question: "Is God my master, or is money my master?" Be honest with yourself. If your answer is that your money has entirely too much control over your life, you're not alone.

Read those verses in Mark 10 one more time. What would it look like to use your money to serve others?

Establish guardrails against greed. To avoid greed and irresponsibility: Give. Save. Live.

PRAYER

Be honest with your heavenly Father about the influence your money has over you. Ask him to lead you to a place where *he* is your master, and money is merely a resource you steward with the purpose of serving others and maximizing your own peace and contentment.

NOTES FOR DISCUSSION QUESTIONS

 On a typical day, how often do you think about money?

This is a simple question designed to help group members begin to think about their relationship with money.

 During the video, Andy defined "greed" as "an assumption that it's all for my consumption." Do you agree with that definition? Why or why not?

Allow group members to disagree. It will help set up a better conversation as you move forward.

 Read Matthew 6:25–27. Why is it challenging to not worry about money? What increases worry about money?

This is the first personal question. Give your group members time to think. The more they recognize the negative effects of worry in their lives, the more helpful the conversation will be as you move forward.

 Why is it often difficult for people to believe that God and the church want something for them and not money from them?

Give group members the space to be skeptical of God and/or the church. Don't argue. Don't try to convince. But don't hesitate to share your own experiences.

 What obstacles have, in the past or present, prevented you from giving first, saving second, and living off the rest? What would keep you from prioritizing giving moving forward?

Give group members time to identify specific obstacles to changing their financial priorities. Be as specific as possible in your own answers.

SESSION FIVE

NOTES FOR LEADING

BOTTOM LINE

What do you usually do to cope with your negative emotions? Do you think your response is healthy? If not, what do you think it would take to adopt a new approach?

TO PREPARE TO LEAD THE FIFTH SESSION:

- Read Proverbs 4:23; Matthew 15:2–7, 10–11, 16–20; and Philippians 4:7. Use the "Reflection" and "Prayer" sections to consider the verses you've read.

- Read the session materials, watch the video, and look through the Discussion Questions.

REFLECTION

What is the current state of your heart? Are you experiencing the "peace of God, which transcends all understanding"? Are you struggling with guilt, anger, greed, or jealousy?

Remember: The heart leaks. Whatever is on the inside will eventually show up on the outside. It will influence your behavior and harm your relationships.

Take action now to establish guardrails around your heart.

PRAYER

Read Proverbs 4:23 as a prayer. Ask God to help you do whatever is necessary to guard your heart.

NOTES FOR DISCUSSION QUESTIONS

 When have you seen someone blow up or lose it over something inconsequential? Knowing that "what comes out of the mouth flows from the heart," what do you think could have really been going on?

This is a simple question designed to help the group think about how they've seen the big idea of this session play out in the world around them.

 Proverbs 4:23 says, "Above all else, guard your heart, for everything you do flows from it." What are some examples of ways "your heart" fuels how you react or behave?

Allow group members to disagree without judgment. It will create a more helpful conversation moving forward.

3 *Jesus stated in Matthew 15:18, "But the things that come out of a person's mouth come from the heart, and these defile them." The relationship between our hearts and our actions is explained with a visual below. Before today's video message, had you considered that your negative behavior is offensive to God?*

Don't rush this part of the discussion. It's not just about group members understanding the relationship between heart and speech, but allowing them to explore that connection and how they've seen it in their lives and the world around them.

4 *Which of the four emotions Andy mentioned is your biggest tendency? Do you relate to any of the "owe" statements?*

☐ Guilt *(I owe you.)*
☐ Anger *(You owe me.)*
☐ Greed *(I owe me.)*
☐ Jealousy *(Life owes me.)*

If you feel comfortable doing so, talk to the group about why you selected the statement(s) you did.

Don't press group members to share, but encourage them to open up by opening up yourself. With which "owe" statements do you identify? Why? Talk about what you've done in the past to try to overcome those tendencies and how successful those strategies have been.

 Andy proposed that some of the people we respect the most are the ones who have endured suffering and pain but have refused to be owned by anger or resentment. Why are those people so impressive?

Be ready with your own example. Be specific about someone you've known who demonstrated extraordinary self-control and how that influenced you.

What Makes You Happy Video Study

It's Not What You'd Expect

Andy Stanley

Everybody wants to be happy. Everybody is on a happiness quest. For many, happiness is measured in moments. Experiences. It's elusive. Unsustainable. What about you? What makes you happy? Something comes to mind for each of us.

In this six-session video Bible study (video sold separately), pastor Andy Stanley examines the ways in which we tend to define *happiness* and explains how that definition influences the way we pursue it. He reveals that happiness is about *who*, not *what*, and that happy people are at peace with God, with others, and with themselves. He also shows how sin undermines peace because it separates us from God, others, and ourselves by substituting pleasure for fulfillment, things for people, images for intimacy, and self-expression for self-control.

We are often tempted to believe that happiness comes from acquiring things, but happiness is actually an outcome of what we sow in our lives. We can't acquire, consume, or exercise our way to happiness, but we may be able to serve and volunteer our way there. In the end, we find that if we live as if it's all about us, we will never be happy.

Sessions include:

1. Nothing
2. Plan for It
3. Peace with God
4. Happy Money
5. Shoes
6. You're Not Enough

Available in stores and online!

Christian Video Study

It's Not What You Think

Andy Stanley

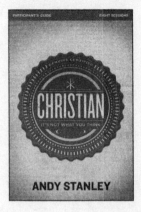

According to Andy Stanley, the words used to describe Christians today often bear no resemblance to what Jesus wanted his followers to be known for.

In this eight-session video study (participant's guide sold separately), you'll learn:

- What one word should be descriptive of every Christian
- How Jesus' followers should treat those who are outside the faith
- Why people love Jesus but can't stand his followers

What does is mean to be Christian? Curiously, the term is never used in Scripture. Instead, Christian was a label used by outsiders to define Jesus' followers. Jesus referenced "disciple" as the key word he used to describe his supporters along with the fact that they would be known for their love—a novel concept for their time—and ours today.

Sessions include:

1. Brand Recognition
2. Quitters
3. Insiders, Outsiders
4. Showing Up
5. When Gracie Met Truthy
6. Angry Birds
7. Loopholes
8. Working It Out

Available in stores and online!

Follow Video Study

No Experience Necessary

Andy Stanley

Lots of people think Christianity is all about doing what Jesus says. But what if doing what Jesus says isn't what Jesus says to do at all? Jesus' invitation is an invitation to relationship, and it begins with a simple request: follow me.

Religion says "Change and you can join us." Jesus says, "Join us and you will change." There's a huge difference. Jesus doesn't expect people to be perfect. He just wants them to follow him. Being a sinner doesn't disqualify anyone. Being an unbeliever doesn't disqualify anyone. In fact, following almost always begins with a sinner and unbeliever taking one small step.

In this eight-session video-based Bible study (participant's guide sold separately), Andy Stanley takes small groups on a journey through the Gospels as he traces Jesus' teaching on what it means to follow.

Sessions include:
1. Jesus Says
2. Next Steps
3. Fearless
4. Follow Wear
5. The Fine Print
6. What I Want to Want
7. Leading Great
8. Unfollow

Available in stores and online!

The New Rules for Love, Sex, and Dating Video Study

Are you the person you are looking for is looking for?

Andy Stanley

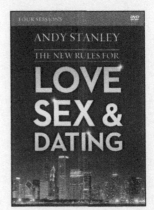

Single? Looking for the "right person"? Thinking that if you met the "right person" everything would turn out "right"? Think again. In this video-based small group Bible study, Andy Stanley explores the challenges, assumptions, and land mines associated with dating in the twenty-first century. Best of all, he offers the most practical and uncensored advice you will ever hear on this topic.

Not for the faint of heart, *The New Rules for Love, Sex, and Dating Video Study* challenges singles to step up and set a new standard for this generation.

> *"If you don't want a marriage like the majority of marriages, then stop dating like the majority of daters!"*
>
> — Andy Stanley

Session Titles

1. The Right Person Myth
2. The Gentleman's Club
3. Designer Sex
4. If I Were You

Available in stores and online!

ZONDERVAN®
.com

Starting Point DVD and Conversation Guide, Revised Edition

A Conversation about Faith

Andy Stanley and the Starting Point Team

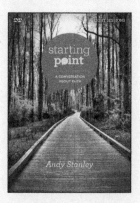

Everything has a starting point—your life, your relationships, your education, your career.

Sometimes we forget that faith has a starting point as well. For some of us, our faith journeys began in childhood as a set of beliefs handed to us by a parent, teacher, or pastor. Maybe you developed a framework of faith based on personal experience. Or maybe you had no faith at all. Too often, a faith formed in childhood isn't strong enough to withstand the pressures of adult life.

But what if you could find a new starting point for faith?

Welcome to Starting Point—an 8-session small group conversation about faith. Whether you're new to faith, curious about God, or coming back to church after some time away, it's a place where your opinions and beliefs are valued, and no question is off limits.

During the eight sessions, you will:

- Use the *Starting Point Conversation Guide* to reflect on central questions of faith and life.
- Watch the video component each week in preparation or as part of the discussion.
- Explore and share what you're learning with other people in a conversational environment.

Come as you are and build relationships with others as you discover your starting point.

Available in stores and online!